Sheltered in Place

poems by

CJ Giroux

Finishing Line Press
Georgetown, Kentucky

Sheltered in Place

for S. and G.

ACKNOWLEDGMENTS

Many thanks to the editors of the journals and websites where the
following poems first appeared:

Caesura: "Quarantined—Trying to Pray"
Connecticut River Review: "Quarantined—Day 15: Shelter in Place"
Ducts.com: "naming the memory ward # 1–9"
Ozone Park: "naming the memory ward #10: blackbird"
Presence: "Quarantined—Shelter in Place: 5th Sunday of Lent"
The Quarantine Chronicles: "Quarantined—Worry in Place: Insomniac's
Alarm"

Much gratitude goes out to the many folks who offered support, advice,
and encouragement in the creation of this collection and the poems found
in it, particularly Grace Giroux, Sally Giroux, Bruce Gunther, Zilka Joseph,
M. L. Liebler, Anne-Marie Oomen, Helen Raica-Klotz, Melissa Seitz, the
faculty and staff of the Bear River Writers' Conference, the faculty and
staff of the Interlochen Creative Writers Retreat, and the editorial staff of
Finishing Line Press.

Publisher: Leah Huete de Maines
Editor: Christen Kincaid
Cover Art: Sally Giroux
Author Photo: Grace Giroux
Cover Design: Elizabeth Maines McCleavy

Order online: www.finishinglinepress.com
also available on amazon.com

Author inquiries and mail orders:
Finishing Line Press
PO Box 1626
Georgetown, Kentucky 40324
USA

Table of Contents

Blizzard, Birth

> *"Saginaw Hospital was founded in 1887 by a group of 24 Saginaw women, despite the doubts of their wealthy husbands and the skepticism of the city's doctors. The women persevered, proposing building a hospital for women and children."*
> —*Covenanthealthcare.com*

I trade scrubs for sweats; overheated hallways for parking lots, falling temps, air heavy with fast-food grease. With my scarf pulled tighter, higher, I nose our Ford Focus into ruts, follow a trail of blurred taillights. Your car seat, unused, awaits. The wipers tick, stick. Snow squalls cyclone across Cooper Street, as I recall moments that remain just ours: *you lifted by the surgeon, your feet first, eyes open; the nurse who took your measurements; the resident who inked your feet, pressed skin to paper and then skin to skin, a temporary tattoo pulsing on my forearm, marking us a tribe of our own.* But now, as I drive home, your footprint, the glow of the ambulance bay are already fading; you, your mom are resting, sleeping, I hope, on this first night. I must wait for tomorrow, so I will my prayers behind me, asking those Fates who taught me to cut your cord, those nymphs who swaddled with pink flannel, to keep watch against the dark, to fill your night with blessings, to baptize you with sterile waters.

naming the memory ward #1

on movie night
where credits never run
nurses push patrons
outdoors
(as if diners would order this dish)

the screen is a sheer sheet
pinholed
white as a pumpkin seed

i imagine edges burning inward
narrowing
to ashes
ashes
ash
sh

Quarantined—Tending the Garden Beds: 4th Sunday of Lent

Leaves of hyacinth, the errant tulip
hide buds, their colors
a secret, a shyness.
Curved petals of sedum
are like feathered fans
unfolding in an old Hollywood musical
to unveil the beauty queen-protagonist—
pearls of dew reflect the silver sky.

Because the wind brings more rain,
I think of the Temple of Santiago
rising from receding reservoirs,
the outline of transept doors curved like cloches:
polished, free of oily fingerprints,
and filled with light.
Santiago's whitewashed walls
erode under time's hard edge.

Like the temple's missing steeple
and cross of greening copper,
the weathervane on my garage
lacks its arrowhead:
north by northeast is
south by southwest,
pointing both to, from masters who love,
the dead who won't rise.
Metal catches metal
under expanding skies;
flakes of rust have fallen
into shingles
their edges curving up like patens;
I think of holy water
sprinkled on the faithful.

In plague times,
loss has its own life.
Seeking days of sun,
I rake last year's lilac leaves,
matted and wet,
on this halfway point
between ashes and Easter—
the dead still won't rise.

Spring, Bliss Park

*"Aaron T. Bliss, governor of Michigan from 1900 to 1904[,]
donated this parkland to the city of Saginaw in 1903.
The Cottage Garden Company of Queens, New York, created
an artistic plan that the made the park seem much larger
than its actual size. The completed park featured two small
brick buildings, more than 2,800 shrubs, vines, trees, and plants.
It has a heart-shaped flower garden as its centerpiece."*
—*Michigan Historical Markers*

The world expands. Moving from the tallest tower of Covenant's complex, from shadow to shade, I push your stroller across the diagonal-lined lawn. We move south-southwest through damp grass clippings. Orange barrels sprout like toadstools; X marks the spot on this city block. Under growing clouds, lilacs brown, bend, rot; denote the perimeter of park space; root the city to its greenhouse past. I run from lightning, into rising wind, over broken bottles, past the wayward blue of chicory. At the picnic shelter, two tables stand on end, leaning against wood posts, like teens outside gym doors too cool for the dance. I lift you up, inhaling the lingering scent of talc; we count sacs of spider eggs, rainbowed graffiti. You look for letters, your name, finding the g and e in *good time*, the c, a, r, more e's in *Charlene*, who is, allegedly, a bitch. I scan for other meaning in the thinning light, see no smile in gang symbols. Thunderheads clamber through a hole in the roof as skies explode.

naming the memory ward #2

another visit
i leave the day's burning eye
adjust to ward walls

a bird in the hand _____
                    poops pecks pleads
it's raining cats _____
                    what
a rose is a rose is a _____
                    flower
don't throw the baby out _____
                    ever

a perfect score
you still lose

Quarantined—Trying to Pray

Yellow construction tape cordons off
the church's main steps;
warnings of caution, danger
curve like a county road in rural Michigan.
Gravel cracks under foot;
open sky is caught in bottle tops—
mirrored circles of dew
surrounded by rusting teeth.

Jailed behind chain link,
like migrants at the Southern border,
the marble mother cradles her child.
His corpse is freckled from city rain.
His open hand hangs,
but hers is a gentle arc, mostly white,
a curved needle, minus thread,
ready for suturing.
Beneath their black plinth,
concrete planters lay on their sides:
white paint peels;
cracking bamboo stakes
shrink like the leg bones
of dead fawns succumbing to the weather.

I want to believe
despite what you have become:
        your thinning body, tapering fingers;
        your name shortened to O Lady of t. Car;
        Sunday service shrunk to m ss a :30.

O Lady of t. Car,
teach me to pray
to the silenced god of second chances
in this rustbelt town where broken glass
falls like seeds on sidewalks;

where diesel fumes coat the air;
where wild chicory grows,
angled, misshapen
out of asphalt.
Stoplights move from red to green
on empty streets,
our corona curfew in place.

Summary, Ojibway Island

> *"[The old Ojibway Island Drive Bridge, a] concrete rigid-frame bridge with original R4 style railings.... is historically significant as an example of a bridge built using Depression programs, and is a documented Works Progress Administration bridge."*
> —HistoricBridges.org

Mats of reeds, current-caught, congregate at shore. We lap Ojibway's one-way loop, collecting colors and animals: crows with the sheen of blue bruises, the woodchuck flattened among clover, the albino kittens we've christened ghost cats. With jokers clipped to clothespins, clicking, you pedal ahead, learning to resist the single training wheel that remains to your right. Off-balance, I try to stay in a jog, stumbling on gravel, rippling potholes. We meet at the bridge below the bridge, new above old, near the granite boulder, grey-streaked, that marks the valley's first Catholic priest. I imagine him—canoed, calling down prayers in French—in this place where winds empty waterways, where the Corps of Engineers sifts silt to free poison. I will you, him, them to slow down where waters rise, to seek wild ramps, the sweetness of purple phlox.

naming the memory ward #3

tvs burn blue
yesterday's menu loops
beef bacon baloney

i carve with sharpies
on polyester
a deflated blouse
blue scarf bursting with begonias

sharp lines bleed
bend
bruises blossom

Quarantined—Checking the Neighbor's House

Suspended from cracked plastic, a souvenir
from Cracow, Irene's key dangles like a pendulum.

The color of overripe plums, the door's enameled surface
evokes Ukrainian Easter eggs—their yolks,

strings of albumen emptied through pinpricks.
The gold-plated knocker waits, its blemishes like age spots.

Schlage, I read and then palm the key, pressing its teeth
into my flesh. *Schlagen*, I recite from memory, *in Bausch und Bogen,*

mit Stumpf und Stiel. Phrases exist, meaning is gone,
but I've remembered the trick of jiggling the lock.

Slipped through the mail slot, Domino's circulars are like flotsam
after the boxcars left the *shtetl.* Offers for credit cards cover octagon
    tiles,

cry "Stop." With handles like question marks, umbrellas
stand guard in the corner, barking "Who goes there?"

Fall, Third-Grade Fieldtrip

*"Welcome to our strolling garden. Its gate opened
in 1971 as designed by Mr. Yataro Suzue and Lori Barber.
He stated then: 'beauty is not trickery, not illusion,...
but arranging elements like trees, water and rocks in a way
that there is no crowding, no competition for attention.'"*
—Japanese Cultural Center, Tea House,
and Gardens of Saginaw

In a lumber baron's granite castle, we learn local lore, geographic quirks
of five rivers flowing north. After lunch, buses belch diesel to shuttle us
past the shuttered Bearinger Building; there, weeds shift fallen bricks,
split like shells of black walnut, now gone, another city stain. We slide
toward Celebration Square, to mauve azaleas, the softness of cherry
blossoms. Light leaks through vellum shades, where lacquered beams
lack nails, where jasmine steams from curved clay necks. You, your
classmates are drawn to swords, out of doors, red footbridges. Gravel
creeks lead to the zoo—wolves call; over-buttered popcorn beckons.
Tatami mats, the river's lap-lap-lapping hold no interest. You move
with your classmates in a pack, just out of my sight. I count heads at
stoplights, follow in an invisible wake.

naming the memory ward #4

photos mark months
scalloped sepia surfaces in september
bridesmaids and bouquets bear blanks
groomsmen grin

you ask their names
i have no answer

so i try to bring the outdoors in
line your windowsill
name what I can
rosemary red basil lavender
love-lies-bleeding
rue

Quarantined—Worry in Place: Insomniac's Alarm

Our male tomcat with one eye
blue, one green
is drawn to the rustling of flannel
sheets, log cabin quilts; he curls into
my side, his purr a low rumble.
We both startle at the 5 AM freight
sounding its horn
of three short bleats;
then another, nearer, higher pitched,
offering three long blasts;
then a third train, farther along.
I'm surprised by the last
in such quick succession,
the deep tenor of its five siren calls.

I imagine these trains on parallel tracks,
the cars passing,
one blue, one green,
one blue, one green,
one blue, one green.
Gaps between Canadian National
Railway, CSX, Norfolk Southern move.
Negative spaces blur, fill, grow;
north, south slant, shift east, west.

Though they've probably passed
the city limits, I think of Emily Dickinson
and iron beasts, viruses stalling in the city:
stopped along switchbacks by the river,
cars wait to uncouple, rejoin with a click,
their sides aglow with neon tags
of local gangs (Southside, Kings),
no alpha, no omega, no
beginning no
end.

Resistance is futile
—engineers remain in control—
but still I dream them on
to a circuit of veins, arteries
pulsing across the continent.
Feverish, short of breath,
a metallic taste on my tongue,
I hear their lonesome cries;
picture their toxic waste,
cargoes of propane,
potential flame elsewhere.

Christmas Walk

"This is a 19.25 mi Bike Ride...
It has a total ascent of 66.37 ft and has a maximum
elevation of 618.24 ft.
TAGS: Bike Path Surface Flat Contour For Workout
Good For Handicap Residential Area River
Surroundings Rural Area Scenic Surroundings
Very Easy Difficulty Very Smooth Terrain"
*   —MapmyRide*

No snow on the rail trail, nor sun, but sparrows, always dust-brown sparrows: they fly from red-twig to birch branch. Pulled from unwrapped presents—from Harry and Hermione, Katniss, another Harry—you refuse to flit. I shiver on splintered benches built with boards, negative space. Your mom winds a wreath from grapevine wilding along the ditch. We wait, watch you crouch, debate whether elm twig or the criss-cross of acorn caps captures your attention. A persistent wind sieves through the net of upper branches. Its dying whistle conjures a ghost train. Your orange jacket is a buoy on this asphalt stream; your pink hat a water lily, tethered, out of season, in a channel linking inland lakes. I look through the growing dusk towards St. Charles, its markers and coal mines. We will never get there, and when I try to narrow the gap, a wayward chickadee, chattering in its black beret, warns me, away, away, away, calling only the faithful to come.

naming the memory ward #5

the change in weather brings baby albums
more snapshots:
another hospital bed
iris pinned to your chest
priests peddle blessings in bottles

even i know their line
(what do you ask of the church)

saints slip
from your tongue
like words from your past

Quarantined—Shelter in Place: 5th Sunday of Lent

As skies open and showers fall, I listen
from my bedroom to today's mass livestream;
the repetition of reading, reading, gospel, homily
is another river moving forward, but a glitch
in transmission sends me back into the lectionary,
like spawning salmon breaking a silver surface,
creating ripples that overlap, cross
in an invisible wake.

The miracle of Martha and Mary's mourning,
the bishop argues again when the video resumes,
was not just a resurrection,
but a return to the land of stones
(and stonings I think for the second time),
the three-day gap between the body's
dying and soul's departure.

I imagine Lazarus waking to lavender,
linen looping his face
like thread on a bobbin,
for rebirth should smell like spring.

But spring is a mere dream:
homes have become caves,
and there is no rock to roll away;
we, too, live behind masks
and raised beds are just cocoons:
the beginnings of snow pea, radish, red kale
have yet to part the soil
framed by peeling paint,
old storm windows that I lower when cold comes.
Sprouting remains a tentative task,
requiring coaxing, forcing.

And the rain seems to never end:
runoff, silt gather along low-lying property lines;
the backyard becomes our own pool of Siloam, pond of sent,
as the maroon crowns of peonies break the surface,
wave to the entangled
stands of last year's clematis
and the drowsing heads of hellebores that look
elsewhere, earthward,
like mourners afraid to show their tears.
Stalks of coneflowers, milkweed rise
like upright pieces of cruciform.
I pray to the God of rescue;
I must stay in place to enter the light.

Modulation, Spring Concert, Mary of the Assumption

"Attracting 3,000 visitors and counting each summer,
Jazz on Jefferson continues to bring great music, food,
heritage and a sense of community to the Saginaw area."
—*CastleMuseum.org*

I walk from day light into cathedral heat. Oiled pews resist the faithful with a squeak; coved ceilings wrap the congregation in sound, the wayward squawk of clarinets. Your mom and I will your smile; you refuse eye contact, the light on your glasses an accomplice, and then, in a rush, you fill our arms with flute case, cardigan, dog-eared music. I hide behind another lens, to pose, focus parent, child. You forget this inconvenience when you wobble away on first heels—you, your classmates seek communion in neon-blue sno-cones, the grit of over-salted fries. As lowriders growl and prowl over bricked streets, backfires mask gunshots. At the baptismal font, I pray for protection, blessing myself, my hand moving up, down, east, west. Before me, music hangs over asphalt like fog. Behind me, Mary travels from Calgary to Cana, from Egypt to Elizabeth, but all I map are sorrowful mysteries.

naming the memory ward #6

you rustle
wrestle with candy wrappers
stripped of sweetness
raspberries resurrecting roommates

surrounded by seagrass
cradled by cotton
you stare to space
succumb

Quarantined—Day 15: Shelter in Place

The first real spring
storms, the forecaster promises,
will pass north, but rising wind
and night skies in the early afternoon
say otherwise, so too our aging
tuxedo cat: growling, bristling,
she has forgotten
that rolling thunder is like the grumbled grievances
of the long-married
muttering to themselves.
The bird that lives on our porch
also sounds her warning;
usually silent, she offers a panicked trill,
a trio of notes,
ending with a whistled *wheat*.

Hidden in the wreath of pinecones
hanging on our storm door,
she sinks into greying bits of lavender,
anise hyssop, thatch, salvia.
My lack of labor last fall has found purpose.
My wife has checked the reference books—
Carpodacus mexicanus, gestation is 14 days—
but I just say mama bird, count eggs
(from three to five, more white
than blue, in a span of 36 hours).
Migration is not an option,
so I text photos to my mother
nesting in place two hours away.

I must refrain from opening up
the interior door, steel painted white,
to the warming April air.
I must stop looking through the window insert
shaped like a wagon wheel—
even reflections, glances frighten.
I must forget about the mess
streaking down the glass,
and learn instead a new vocabulary:
finch, not bird,
Russian sage, not waste,
hope, not fear;
though I am not alone,
I must shelter in shadow.

Another Fall, Potter Street Station

> *"We must preserve that which our forefathers left in trust
> for us to pass on to future generations for their awareness
> and appreciation of their ancestors."*
> —PotterStreetStation.com

Dreaming of red winter wheat, the yellow pinwheels of Jerusalem artichokes in bloom, I leave Abele's Greenhouse. Perennials on my mind, I ease along Veterans' Parkway, past First Ward, the GM Casting Plant. I pause at Potter Street Station—grieve its sagging turrets, bending beams, molding walls. In this floodplain of poverty, chained link grows; barbed wire blooms; no standing signs rise like weeds, but trains, transmission plants are gone. You too remain elsewhere, no interest in errands. Seeking patterns in cracked panes, angry over missing glass and the absent, I contemplate angles, the need for distance. With the car idling, engine pinging, I pace, rattle the fence, consider my aim. I collect cement stones, calculate their weight, shift them from palm to palm.

naming the memory ward #7

patient/guest/in/out
impatient/outguess
outing/out/in
i refuse the visitor log
blaming blooms in my fingers

christmas cacti burn blood-red at easter

Quarantined—Crossing the Threshold (Back to the Neighbor's)

Between the French door before me,
its paint crackling, and the exterior one behind,

I conjure airlocks, space travel, long flights overseas,
the stale recycled air, cigarette smoke.

The furnace kicks in with a rush, hiss, whiff of gas.
My coat zipped, I remember trips to JL Hudson's

Department Store, now gone, where uniformed attendants,
also gone, announced each floor. Their gloves whiter

than fiberglass snow, their gold buttons glistening like stars,
they marked the way to Santa's Workshop, women's wear, home
    furnishings.

Flies freckle the frosted glass, silver leafing of the overhead light.
Though I am alone, I pull my mask higher,

imagine papery carcasses rustling
as they shift under the single bulb that still burns.

Another Winter, Shiawassee National Wildlife Refuge

*"Shiawassee National Wildlife Refuge was established in 1953
and contains more than 9,800 acres of marsh, bottomland
hardwood forest, and grasslands... within an agricultural and
urban landscape."*
—*U.S. Fish & Wildlife Service*

I still have not learned the park's seasons. The driving trail has been
closed for weeks, so we circle the lot, walking the uneven planks of
observation decks. Placards herald ring-necks, swans, red-breasts.
We remain divided, trading Taylor Swift for swifts and hard frost,
bleached photos for cattails and moss-green ponds. I look ahead
to other times: the long expanse of wrinkled blue; sunning shades
of cormorants; the rare return, perhaps, of the American white
pelican. Above us, eagles nest; around us, embankments are bound
by prairie grass. You move to your own equinox, solstice.

naming the memory ward #8

i stake mums in shade
twist twine
to tether stalk to stick

i brush against obedient plants
belled blooms
feathered ferns
poison ivy

pinked petals elongate
into empty-eyed needles

phones stay still

i transplant aster after aster
asterisk sunburst

diagnoses await

Quarantined—Shelter in Place: Second Octave of Easter

Insomnia grows like haloes
ringing our neighborhood: street-
lights, porchlights, the dusk-
to-dawns color the cul-de-sac,
glowing like orange pushpins
plotting the pandemic.

Baptized by the blue
screen of my iPad,
I watch today's online service;
the first reading is no longer Old
Testament, and the gospel
miracle, the bishop says,
is of presences unseen, the scales
falling from eyes, but I am distracted
by email tabs, symptoms, to-do lists,
the thought of green
mold that grows on our paling yellow siding.

The Lyrids remain a myth;
the quivering Northern Lights,
another legend this far south,
undulate beyond closed eyes.
Today's gift is that Emmaus
(out of sight, unknown) nears;
hearts still burn;
the sun still rises.

Another Summer, Huntington Event Park

"A city's struggles do not paint a picture of its identity....
The glorious red brick, Chicago School-inspired, six-story
[Bearinger Fireproof Building]—replete with atrium,
marble work, and brass fixtures and oak trim—has been
on the National Register of Historic Places since 1982."
    —John Horn, "Saved from the Ball: Entrepreneurs Revive
    Historic Buildings," SecondWaveMedia.com

We sink into steel shade, nylon camp chairs, as the Eddy Band wrings songs from reed, metal, moist air. I tap my foot to selections from *Wicked, Star Wars*, even Prince. You lament the grey-haired audience, the damp bread of your tuna fish sandwich, your parents' presence. Gnats spiral over the lawn; storms clouds sidle closer. I wish away the impending rain despite this season of drought, count the windows along the Bearinger Building's top floor. Its blinds slant toward the river, the crumbling breakwall. I wonder whether black Vs swooping over pavilion eaves are bats or birds; question where they nest; imagine guano etched onto cracking plaster, oak, marble. Whatever the number, whatever the species, I know you will say I am wrong.

naming the memory ward #9

today i may be your father brother uncle
wearing blue
bringing forget-me-nots
acquiescing
allowing
agreeing
telling you go go
go

Quarantined—Day 44: Nesting in Place

My wife informs me, on her birthday,
of nest removal laws, that hoping means waiting,
but like Thomas in the upper room,
I hope a little less.

Still, with my makeshift mask of tessellating geese in flight
and nitrile garden gloves that glow like a Baltimore oriole,
I move out of doors, from flowerbed to flowerbed:
iris to cranesbill, hyacinth to parrot tulip.

In the shade of our front porch, eggs still number five,
but grow thinner, paler, dimmer.
The finches have fled their cup of thatch still
scratching the glass, still moved by spring storms.

Brown seeds of white pine are splayed
like splintered ribs. I clear away standing spines
of milkweed stalk, their wooden cradles of seedpods.
I think of flames, but Pentecost is a dream, a lifetime away.

After pruning the dead ends of the holly, the lone wild rosebush
and its crown of thorns, I turn to the blackened needles
of purple coneflower that we overwinter for chickadees,
cardinals, those who still migrate north.

I must lower my mask to free
bifocals of fog: exhalation and insight are at odds.
Removing my gloves to pull slivers from my fingers,
I expect blood—but no stigmata—and leave the shelter in place.

Still Summer, Back to the Shiawassee

*"Shiawassee Refuge is designated as a United States Important
Bird Area for its global significance to migratory waterfowl."*
    —*U.S. Fish & Wildlife Service*

We drag you back to the preserve in our station wagon, its rust older
than your 13 years. Armed with sweatshirts, peach tea, popcorn, we
rumble past the litter of Lanny's Resale. Gravel crunches under balding
treads. Snowy egrets, golden warblers, green-winged teals are night
nesting, save a single silhouette on the bayou's tallest trunk. Stripped
of twig, bark, branch, it rises like a tuning fork. Rangers lament light
pollution; astronomers press eyes to glass, offer Saturn's icy rings to us.
On the car's cooling hood, we lean against glass damp with dew. The
darkness deepens. You speak of Polaris, Pegasus, the Pleiades, and then
spy your first, second, third meteor, there, there, there, gone. I think of
outstretched wings, remember Roman martyrs. On the midnight drive
back through town, I see you there, there, there, gone.

naming the memory word #10: blackbird

redwing blackbird slices through the may air
past the sitting room's glass
to rest on a roadside cattail

reed bends, asphalt-bound
hovering over
the remains of yesterday's downpour

scarlet and saffron markings glow
like a new tattoo
like a match raised towards a newly rolled cigar
and I recall the photo found while packing

you had transplanted yourself to california
a summer trip with a girlfriend
the war, high school over

knott's berry farm is penciled in the white scalloped margin
you, your unidentified classmate stand
side-by-side
(starched peasant-sleeves
peter pan collars, sepia tones)

in makeshift capris, cork-screwed curls
you mug for the camera
thumbs lifted to hitch a ride

you wing your way into a black-and-white future
dreaming of color

Quarantined—Sign Park: Completing the Circuit

I imagine lying, without you,
in a virus-free summer, on browning islands
of Kentucky rye, cropped too short,

surrounded by asphalt, broken glass,
what once was Southern comfort:
short-lived, divine.

As gables, rooms become vacant again,
neon red leads to neon green, block letters
connecting like tenement halls, mildewed.

Brenske's Plumbing burns
electric pink in August skies,
hides Lyra, Cygnus, St. Lawrence's intermittent tears.

The leaky faucet drips Earl Grey, sympathy
from Sagittarius' kettle—a drop there, there, there,
gone and then lower: there, there, there,

gone, and once more, following its dictated path
into my waiting mouth, opened,
always wanting sweetness, more.

CJ Giroux was born and raised in Michigan. He grew up in the metropolitan Detroit area and completed his studies at Wayne State University. His dissertation focused on representations of trauma in the works of twentieth-century African American dramatists. He is a professor of English at Saginaw Valley State University, where he also helped direct the school's Writing Center and served as co-director of its Center for Community Writing. He is one of the founding editors of the community literary arts journal *Still Life* and the author of the chapbook *Destination, Michigan.* His poems can be found in journals and anthologies in the U.S. and abroad. He also serves on the staff of *Dunes Review.*

CPSIA information can be obtained
at www.ICGtesting.com
Printed in the USA
JSHW020346160822
29264JS00003B/204